WEST OF WEST

By the same author

The Jerusalem Guide
The Jerusalem Folio
Cork (with Eilean Ní Chuilleanáin)
Dublin Ninety Drawings
Kilkenny City and Topography
Voices from Stones
The Myth of Icarus
Dublin Bay

Brian Lalor studied at the Crawford Municipal School of Art, Cork, and subsequently in England and Greece. He worked in architecture for a number of years and then became involved in archaeology, acting as a specialist on ancient buildings on French, British, American and Israeli excavations. From 1974 he concentrated on art and came to live in West Cork. He ran an art gallery in Schull, exhibiting the work of some of the many artists who lived in the area, and he has had his own work exhibited in Ireland, Europe and the USA. In his writing he is fascinated by history—at once a burden and a gift—and by the interweaving of the present and the past.

WEST *of* WEST

AN ARTIST'S ENCOUNTER WITH WEST CORK

Brian Lalor

BRANDON

Thanks to Peggie Jordan, Christine MacDonald, Willie Olsen, Birgitta Saflund, Wendy Smith.
In memory of Commandant Stephen Lalor 1900–61.

First published in 1990 by
Brandon Book Publishers Ltd
Cooleen, Dingle, Co. Kerry

Text and Etchings © Brian Lalor 1990

British Library Cataloguing in Publication Data
Lalor, Brian
    West of west: an artist's encounter with West Cork.
    1. Cork (County). Description & travel
    I. Title
    914.19504824

    ISBN 0-86322-109-2

This book is published with the financial assistance of The Arts Council/An Chómhairle Ealaíon, Ireland

Cover designed by The Graphiconies
Typeset by Irish Typesetting and Publishing Ltd, Galway
Printed by Richard Clay Ltd, Bungay, Suffolk

Contents

WEST CORK

WELL MET BY MOONLIGHT

Nor must the painter forget long black tracts of bog
here and there, and the water glistening brightly at the
places where the turf has been cut away.

W.M. THACKERAY **The Irish Sketch Book**, 1843

DRIVING WITH MY WIFE in our ancient and quixotic estate car on a late November evening, we left the main Cork-Bantry road at Buckley's shop and set off up an unpromising by-road flanked by wild blackthorn hedges. A mile up the road the lights of the car failed. It was eleven o'clock at night and neither house nor signpost was to be seen, but the darkness was not total once one's eyes became accustomed to the gloom. Dim shapes could be distinguished, and when the moon was not obscured by clouds the landscape took on a weird and spectral beauty. A decision was required: would we return to the forty-watt beacon of Buckley's and enquire for a mechanic, or would we go on, with ten miles to drive over unfamiliar roads? In the past people had travelled only when nature conspired with human intentions. We continued our journey by moonlight.

The road wound away into the distance, a ribbon of reflected light, and the weaving shapes of the blackthorns threw a black Gothic tracery across the landscape. The immediate surroundings had a silvery sharpness, the precision of a lunar landscape; brightly outlined walls enclosed pools of darkness. We were no longer at the door to West Cork but in its very interior. We had arrived.

The landscape of the mind, which co-exists, interlocks and overlaps with the geographer's version, is an intangible, ephemeral thing. You may encounter it unexpectedly on a moonlit night or on some deserted headland, or perhaps in the dim light of a public bar. In this part of the world, soaked in the memories and half-memories of the past, much is implied rather than stated. Like the collective unconscious, the landscape, too, is composed of a multitude of intertwining details. This collection of etchings of West Cork is concerned with those details: with small corners of towns and villages, with oddly-shaped fields and erratic skylines. Each etching is a vignette of landscape, architecture or environment. The pictures are organized around a number of themes yet the material as a whole has such an overall unity that what illustrates one section also has relevance for another. The point which they make is a collective one.

The geographic area which I am concerned with here is bounded on the south and west by the coastline running from Kinsale to Bantry and inland by a line drawn between Cork and Gougane Barra, with the occasional excursion beyond these borders. More particularly, I have focused on the coastal settlements as they represent both the normal and the peculiar in the region, and embody a character distinctive from the areas further away from the sea. The etchings I have made of this place do not – indeed, could not – cover the subject comprehensively; however, each plate shows a fragment characteristic of the south-western perimeter of Ireland over the last twenty years.

Pictures of West Cork in an earlier era are few in the extreme. Unfortunately, this area of the country failed to gain the attention of artists during the nineteenth and early twentieth centuries when so much of the west coast was being painted. Our received image of the West of Ireland owes a great deal to the vision and perception of Paul Henry, Jack B. Yeats, and a whole school of painters who extended the range and depth of this image. Lone artistic voices did of course exist in West Cork – Edith Somerville in Castletownshend and Robert Gibbings in Bandon – but their energies were principally concentrated elsewhere. The records which do exist tend to be repetitive of subject and rarely represent the material adequately. In the 1830s and early '40s an individual location such as Gougane Barra was recorded in various media and by artists of widely varying calibre, from a spirited watercolour by the antiquarian-artist, George Petrie, to the rather grubby little steel engravings in the Halls' travel books. And while the illustrations in the *Dublin Penny Journal* are fairly reliable when dealing with the home counties of the east coast, by the time one gets to West Cork they look as if they had been observed, distantly and narrowly, through the lens of a rather indistinct telescope. The eighteenth-century school of Irish landscape painting, which has left so beautiful a record of the country of eastern and southern Ireland, has little to show for the remote south-west. Even those stalwart sources of journeyman draughtsmanship, the gentleman and lady amateurs, seem to have been remarkably idle. Too busy sighting the French, no doubt.

The strongest impression we have of West Cork in the past comes from two sources: the pictorial journalism of such periodicals as the

Illustrated London News and the vast photographic record of the Lawrence Collection of the late nineteenth century. When some of my etchings are compared with the views taken by Robert French for Lawrence, not a great deal appears to have altered during the intervening century. This is, of course, only partially true: great social and political upheavals have occurred and economic prosperity has generated a major revolution in living standards. But, ignoring for the moment the modern bungalow boom, little fundamental change has come to the fabric of the towns and villages, which achieved their visual apogée around 1890. They are now faced with the choice of preserving that character or succumbing to the only apparent alternative – which is already blighting the countryside around the towns – of a new style sired by the Costa del Sol and middle-American suburbia. This riot of arcades in stucco, Mediterranean tiling, and a sense of *horror vacui* filled by the gnome department of the local garden centre, leaves one returning to the severe lines and rhythmical proportions of the traditional architecture with an acute sense of pleasure. Better the plain and wholesome diet of the past than a feast of visual bonbons.

The subjects of my etchings are certainly plain and wholesome. Stone walls, slate roofs and timber windows all contribute to an ambience which is entirely local, a product of the place, and needing little of the outside world for its continuance. Not the hidden Ireland, for such characteristics are to be found all over the country. More the essential Ireland, timeless and reserved, not given to brash statement but rather acting as a backdrop for the drama, a foil for turbulent skies and the constantly changing patterns of light and shade which perpetually transform all that is before you.

The key to appreciating the particular character of the West Cork region is to develop an awareness of its sense of scale. Observing the individual details which go to make up the whole is an integral part of that understanding. Large, extravagant gestures are rare in poor and marginal areas of any society and are hardly to be expected here, and when found they are expressions of individual whim. Many centuries of poverty and insecurity, of making do, are too ingrained in the emotional make-up to be easily set aside by unaccustomed prosperity.

Contemporary economic categories – the 'relevant consumer' or the 'throwaway society' – have made poor inroads here. The rule, rather, is functionalism above all: nothing should be wasted, everything should find another use once its original purpose has been exhausted. Anything which comes to hand will serve the purpose: a bed-end or some redundant joists will block a gap; an old Morris Minor, toppled on its side, will make an unbudgeable obstacle for wandering cattle. The concept of recycling is nothing new here.

One of the most common features of the area, an area endowed by nature with far more than its fair share of boulders, are the stone walls and fences which border most roads and divide up the land. Standing erect like skeletal fingers emerging from the soil, laid flat like bricks, or matted in strange and purposeful patterns, they career all over the hills, marking territory, enclosing livestock, decorating the barren wastes while attempting to subdue and control its wild contours. The great pre-Christian stone forts which occur along the west coast of Ireland have these same walls, more massive and clearly defensive, yet products of the same craftsmen's skill and mastery of the native stone of their areas. Only a society with an abundance of manpower could have marked their land in so exacting and tortuous a manner. Across mountains, from base to summit and down the other side, a thin line of wall will meander its way, miles of stone apparently enclosing only the wind which whistles over the bogs. Yet nothing is haphazard; each stone is laid with care, and there are filigree sections to let the wind through.

All these small manifestations of care interest me – the well-placed Commer van wedged between gateposts, the carefully angled bed-end lashed to a sapling with binder twine – and seem worthwhile subjects for drawings.

The more general perception of my calling was nicely defined by a local curate. Happening on each other in a Cork back-street, we both stopped but, never having spoken to one another before, were at a loss for a conversational opener. His contribution came first. With a glance at the pad under my arm he remarked breezily, 'Ah, Brian, still scribbling'.

Yes, still.

The Skeaghnore Scarecrow

Ardura by Moonlight

On the Banks of the Leamawadra

Market Street, Kinsale

Rock Garden

Cloud Cover

Rocks & Ivy, Sheds at Rossard

The Crooked Mile

THE LAND OF HEART'S DESIRE

So Geographers in *Afric*-Maps
With Savage-Pictures fill their Gaps;
And o'er unhabitable Downs
Place Elephants for want of Towns.

JONATHAN SWIFT **On Poetry, A Rhapsody,** 1733

THREE OR MORE CENTURIES ago, before the landscape of West Cork became bound by a web of roads and fences, its contours would have been best understood when seen from above, from the heights of Mount Kidd or Mount Gabriel. Parallel ribs of rocks and hills, dividing up the pasture land, extended from the base of the mountains to the coast, where long fingers of rocky promontories projected out into the sea. There was a natural order to everything.

Defining the high spots in the ribs of land, and distributed with apparent regularity all over this landscape, were lush green rings. Single, and occasionally double or triple concentric rings of grassy banks, these features resembled a giant's game of quoits, forgotten and left to decorate the landscape. The gargantuan quoits are of course the ring forts or fairy rings of the Irish countryside, and outlined the form taken by the rural farmsteads and dwellings from pre-Christian times down to the sixteenth century. Each ring represented an earthen rampart on high ground, with perhaps a dry moat or further rampart encircling some wattle huts. Simple and utilitarian, this form of dwelling satisfied the political and practical exigencies of the day – or aeon, for that matter. Rural life was lived in the midst of the land, without congregating in towns or villages.

Looking from a height now, the meandering growth of blackthorn hedges, outcrops of trees, afforestation and the improving hand of man have begun to obscure the ring-game. Bulldozers, land-improvement incentives and progress have all conspired to diminish or destroy the evidence of the past. What dominates the landscape today are the white- and cream-painted farmhouses designed to a standard form, each surrounded by a protective cluster of trees. Their distribution seems arbitrary and again suggests the scatterings of a capricious hand, but in fact the principle is still the same. Instead of clustering together for protection or community each farmyard stands as the core around which the fields are gathered, maintaining its position at the heart of the land just as its circular predecessor did a thousand years before.

'I wonder who lives in that house?'

Through the driving rain a few acres of lush green contrast brightly with the reds and browns of the bracken away up on the side of a bleak mountain. In the midst of the fields one can see the solid bulk of the farmhouse. Behind the house the darker green of a shelter-belt contrasts with the fresh colour of the cultivated fields. Against this mass of dark conifers the house has a bleached and pristine look about it, even through the screen of wind and rain.

Down below in the valley and on the foothills the criss-cross of the field boundaries shows a more intense human presence. The houses are bright specks of washed stonework gleaming in the occasional shaft of sunlight. They seem to grow out of the land and all are surrounded by varying arrangements of the same parts: the ruins of an earlier stone dwelling, now roofless; diminutive stone-built slated sheds and, behind them, the hay-barn with its contrasting barrel-vaulted shape. The nineteenth-century photographs of villages and farms show an unrelieved grimness of stone, cement and clay. Whitewash relieves this picture, though frequently this rendering has degenerated into a leprous greyness indicative of neither hope nor prosperity. Colour has a symbolic relationship with the state of economics in rural Ireland. The last twenty years have seen the introduction of modern synthetics, bringing vivid tones not previously to be found here. Affluence and the EC have brought, as to the Aegean, a flight from the spartan virtues of white and cream, indicating perhaps a fall from grace in rural life at either end of the Mediterranean.

'But, who *does* live in that old farmhouse?'

One day, searching for a ring fort which from the Ordnance Survey map looked of particular interest, I came on a house at the end of an overgrown and rutted track. In the country the stranger is forever asking directions as signposts are virtually unknown away from the main roads. The principle behind the absence of signposts appears to be that 'anyone interested in the old thing would know where it is already'. The house I had come to had the air of having always been at the end of something, never pivotal to even that epitome of rural belonging, the townland. Why had it been built there, below an almost perpendicular cliff and only approachable through a track strewn with boulders? Unanswered questions, and indeed it appeared quite sensibly to have long ago been abandoned. Even so, I banged on the door, and the ancient paintwork fell away in flakes. My knock echoed hollowly through the house; no dog barked, nor did any living thing stir as I turned to go. I assumed it was yet another empty farmhouse whose occupants had peopled the Irish diaspora, preserving the sentiments of home yet realistically eschewing the dream of return.

I retraced my steps through the rutted yard and like Lot's wife involuntarily turned to look back. I detected a slight movement at a window beside the door and was turned to ice rather than salt by what I saw. There was a face, pale and fearful, staring from the darkness within. Taken aback by this apparition I hesitated, and saw at once that each window of the house, so silent and closed, was occupied by a face, aged, worn and colourless. Male, female: I couldn't tell. They gazed in a disembodied way from the interior darkness of the house out at the bright sun of an early summer's day. Aghast at what I had disturbed I retreated down the track, imagining that I heard the slow shuffling of ancient feet as the strange, androgynous hermits of this lost valley returned to their perches and silence resumed its rule.

The isolation inherent in the wide dispersion of farms has both positive and negative aspects. It engenders loneliness, certainly, but also gives those of a more thoughtful nature time to speculate on the world's strange ways, to think about life and achieve some balance. Also, it gives room to fantasize and develop bizarre notions of the why and wherefore of things. In the course of bicycle trips though the countryside I encountered many strange ideas, or rather, encountered concepts somewhat at variance with those more commonly held. To the farmer who has spent his whole life tending thirty recalcitrant acres of rough land in an isolated valley the world is a distant and foolish place, but also fascinating. Working on the land in a traditional way gives one an opportunity to remove oneself from the trivia of the world, as well as from its more central forces. Concepts which have preoccupied whole populations in Europe can have as little currency in the remote West of Ireland as they might have in the Arctic Circle. The Second World War, Flower Power, the invention of photography – these are distant matters involved in other, distant and not quite real worlds.

A farmer, assuming that I am German because many have settled in the area, purchasing previously unsaleable land or ruins, engages me in conversation. Perhaps he has half an acre of rock to sell.

'Hitler was a very good man.'

I bristle slightly at this opening and hope that a panegyric on the Third Reich will not follow it. There is silence, so I venture a question.

'Why do you say that?'

'Sure didn't he put up the price of turf with his war?'

This had to be conceded even if it represented a rather revisionist stance on the question. From this point of view it would have been a good time to have had shares in the boot-polish industry. The perspective of Scarteenakilleen is not that of Coventry or Dresden.

As you sit in a field, drawing or painting the landscape, it can be rather disquieting to realize that someone is watching you from the obscurity of a gorse thicket. Time not being important, observing the artist can be indulged in as a leisurely activity, requiring no participation or any other form of involvement. It is a true spectator sport. When the picture is completed I pack up my equipment and proceed towards the field gate knowing that the scrutineer in the thicket will now emerge with his question. Obliquely, the conversation starts with the weather, proceeds through local geography towards the personal, and eventually arrives at the particular. The real interest is, what have I been doing?

'You've been taking a snap, I see.'

This concept, borrowed from the Box Brownie era, assumes that all the artist has to do is hold up his paper or canvas to the view, say 'presto', and there it all is, magically transformed. By divine or scientific intervention the scene has been rendered onto paper. This viewpoint implies an ascendancy of photography over art which I find most irritating, as it dispenses with effort, skill or artistry. Whistler's snap of his mother, the 'arrangement in black and grey', is much diminished by the term. Often, a neighbouring farmer might say to me, 'Young Carol was down in the haggard taking a snap of me stacking hay'. Translated, this means that the artist in question had probably spent four hours doing a painstaking watercolour of the subject. But what's a few hours to a lifetime spent in the fields? A mere snap!

The further up the mountain people live, the older and more alone they are, the longer it takes for news of the events of the outside world to percolate upwards to their remote fastnesses. Not everyone has a radio or TV, even today, and the information broadcast may in any case be unintelligible to one who has spent a lifetime with animals for companionship and hills for neighbours. The events of the local town and village are the important news, the doings of nearby townlands are the breath of life. New blood is always of interest; new people moving into houses not lived in for thirty, fifty, a hundred years, a fascinating phenomenon. Memory is long in country places and that memory is of repeated departures; of many going and no one except the old coming back. And so it came as an inexplicable shock when in the 1960s lights began to come on in cottages and farmhouses long left derelict, the homes hitherto of marauding cattle and nesting rooks. The new occupants did not even come from familiar places like Boston, Chicago or Camden Town, but from unknown parts with no connotations of blood or bond. Bremen, Bristol, Amsterdam: strange places and strange names. What could it mean? A new influx could only be judged in terms of its predecessors but the comparison was not very enlightening. The Cromwellians were fierce but these newcomers were docile, the Huguenots industrious and these folk idle, the tourists rich and these evidently quite poor. How should it be understood? The strangers were certainly a problem. Their fellow nationals, Colonel and Mrs Gore, now retired from the British Colonial Service, and Herr Piltz, the businessman from Hamburg, who were foreign also and had built holiday homes in the area, did not by their way of life seem to belong to the same nations as the new influx. There was a more fundamental difference.

Driving with my family on a winter's day before Christmas in the foothills of Mount Gabriel, in pursuit of a free-range turkey from a fabled turkey woman, we lost our way in the by-roads. The turkey woman was a Mrs O'Driscoll and as there were many of that name we were soon confused by too many directions. Stopping to enquire at a farmhouse we were confronted with the problem of whether it was Mrs Michael John O'Driscoll or Mrs Tommy Tim O'Driscoll, or one of the many more variations on this clan theme, that we sought. Unenlightened, we passed further and further into the maw of the mountain and the elusive Christmas bird continued to evade discovery.

Twilight had come, the maze of roads seemed indecipherable, the turkey had escaped capture and so, the quest abandoned, we took another turn towards what we hoped might be the direction of the main road. Out of a field gate and onto the roadway emerged an old man of aboriginal appearance, obviously at one with every blackthorn bush and moorhen in this remote place. He would certainly know all the O'Driscolls, and the one we wanted. Stopping and rolling down the window, I waited for him to approach. When he reached us he looked into the car with the transfixed expression of the shepherds who had seen the star. He scrutinized the occupants with an intent and purposeful gaze, absorbing all the details of bearded driver, curiously dressed women and unkempt children in mis-matched clothes sitting in the back. The satisfaction of discovery proclaimed itself on his face and, with the formality of Stanley encountering his quarry on Lake Tanganyika, he said, 'Would ye be hippies?'

The modern farmer with his tractor, silage pit and chemical farming, however much he may be the creature and slave of market forces and farm-grant systems decided on in Brussels and Luxembourg, is at any rate a symbol of progress, although perhaps of a dubious kind. Also, he does represent the majority. The minority position is held by those who have not yet entered the twentieth century – the old and the old-fashioned; and held more vocally by those who have decided to leave it – the refugees from progress and the life of materialism. 'Drop outs' they used to be called, now 'the alternative society', 'New Age people', 'freaks', 'hippies', the last a term of disparagement. The new immigrants, whose lights shine from the previously dark windows of many reclaimed and revived West

Cork farmhouses, have rejected the conventional lives of their parents in favour of a rustic idyll, in timescale located in Hardy's Wessex, though bolstered by social welfare and, like Billy Bunter, 'postal orders from the Pater' at convenient intervals. The answer to the question, 'And who lives there?' is likely to be, 'Oh, some foreigner. Strangers to these parts'.

Hardy's Wessex was peopled by women of strong character and great capacity. The women of the immigrant group tend towards the same virtues: bearing children, baking bread, turning their hands to dairying, craftwork – any task demanded by frontier life. The menfolk are more purely decorative: handy for rolling a joint, fathering a child, claiming welfare. A generalization certainly.

Sue and Mike met at a College of Art in London. They taught for a while, wandered for a longer period, then came to rest in a ruined farmhouse in West Cork. They believed in living the life which the pre-Raphaelites painted, though not quite to the extent of *The Scapegoat*.

It is January, and the harsh life of the pioneer in deepest West Cork is in one of its demanding phases. She crouches over the embers of the previous day's fire, trying to coax it back to life. The chimney-breast is deep enough for a person to sit inside it, and above the fire is suspended the traditional cooking apparatus, the crane, blackened with smoke and age and hung with a large witch's cauldron. Pots of different shapes and sizes are stacked around the fireplace. The floor is pockmarked and damp, its concrete surface glistening with a dew-like sheen of moisture. In bare feet she crosses the unfriendly surface, engaged in her morning routine. Breakfast consists of her own bread baked in the bastable pot, oatmeal porridge, and milk from a herd of Anglo-Nubian goats whose bells could be heard tinkling as they moved around in their shed waiting to be let out. They would graze on the heather and brambles on the mountain till she went for them at dusk.

When the children have set off for school two miles down the road, she puts on her boots and anorack to go and release the goats and poultry, and notices that a blocked drain is flooding the vegetable garden. Resolving to attend to this at once, she returns to the house, prepares some dough in readiness for when the fire is hot; then, listening for sounds of life from upstairs and hearing none, she takes shovel and pick and makes her way out again to the offending drain. The job begun the previous season had not been properly finished and now with the flash-floods of winter the sides are caving in and blocking the flow pouring down from the high land above the house. The rest of the morning is occupied by this task and, in between, tending the fire and baking the bread. Work for a man, the neighbours would say, but she enjoys its slow rhythms, thrusting the shovel deep into the wet earth, with the rasping sound of steel on stone, and heaving the muck up on the bank. At length she is rewarded by a trickle of water in the bottom of the drain, and then a rush as the obstruction is removed.

Returning to the warmth of the house, the fire burning cheerfully and the chimney not smoking for a change, she sits by the heat, grateful for a moment to think without the demands of animals, children, her man, the land. Is that the right order? she wonders.

Having heard the door banging and the thud of booted feet making their way up the muddy garden path, he slowly sits up and glances out through the tiny window to see if it is still raining. Black clouds race up high in the sky and the wind suggests showers rather than heavy rain. Later, in the loft at the other end of the building, he adjusts the wick of the oil-lamp and looks around for a point at which to begin. Canvasses stacked against the walls represent five years of sporadic work, between digging turf, working as a barman in Ryan's lounge bar and grocery, labouring on the afforestation, and sundry other digressions. Digressions from his reason for being here in this hovel trying to reconstruct life as it might have been in a better age, before arts councils and aggression entered the artist's life.

The canvas on the easel shows the family and friends on an idyllic autumnal afternoon, painted in a minute and finely-detailed manner. The goats, chickens and other animals at one with the human young, the loaves and fishes no less miraculous than those of Tiberias, and the fresh faces of the New Age forming the dominant feature of the large canvas. With the occasional scrape of steel on stone reaching him from outside to discomfit his composure, he begins to paint in the flickering light of the lamps, putting in a cluster of mushrooms in the foreground and a pine marten on a branch. He thinks he might call it 'The Peaceable Kingdom'.

The anthropologist need not go to the Amazon Basin or Papua New Guinea in search of odd forms of human existence when they abound in all corners of Europe. They cling to cracks and crevices in the modern world, lurking in alleyways and marooned on mountains.

When I came to live in a remote area of West Cork which no stranger had previously penetrated, I was a source of great local speculation. An old woman who lived alone sent word by a neighbour that she would like to meet the strangers. A visit to her cottage followed this invitation – or command. The house was of the type common to the region, whitewashed and unadorned, two storeys with chimneys at either end of a slated roof. A door flanked by two tiny windows, with three even smaller ones above, made up the facade. At each gable an extension had been added which made a symmetrical and pleasing composition, shaded by mature trees and flanked by various other structures. The house itself was in a fairly alarming state of decay, its door permanently open, tottering on its rusty hinges. The old woman, now a withered crone, was known in the locality for the independence of her mind and the sharpness of her tongue. Years of hard work had left her twisted and arthritic but her mind and will were undimmed. However, the prevailing impression was not of her age and condition but of the overpowering stench of unwashed humanity.

The arboreal gloom of her cottage was a perfect setting for an Irish Kitchen Tragedy or, in a more modern context, for one of those photographs of the abandoned old which charitable societies publish next to the 'Eating Out' columns in certain Sunday papers. Intended as a source of light, the window was caked with layers of grime and the floor was covered in a lifetime's collection of newspapers compressed into a food-mottled linoleum of stale news. The walls – chief feature of the cave – were so densely crowded with faded pictures of saints and defunct popes, ravaged press-cuttings and other memorabilia that it rivalled the Pitti Palace for sheer abundance. In the midst of this den the old woman, now three-quarters blind, hobbled about displaying her treasures for the strangers, each manifestation adding to the surreal tragedy of the place. Two books, severely gnawed around the edges, were produced for inspection. One, a coverless tome, was a history of Catholicism in America, its pages replete with Irish faces in unsmiling sepia. The second, a slim and much read book of the 1930s, related with many photographs the story of the Dionne quintuplets. To the childless, this phenomenon of fruitfulness must have been a source of vicarious motherhood of fabulous degree. The two books were passed into my hands, triumphs of faith and procreation. Like a hermit in the deserts of Nubia giving his treasured manuscripts to a traveller from the West, she pressed them on me saying, 'As a man of education you'll know their worth'.

The tour of the Pitiful Palace continued. Upstairs, having negotiated the creaking and dangerous staircase with an odiferous pail at its turning, we entered successively three tiny bedrooms, one still in use, the other two enmeshed in sheets of spiders' webbing. She showed the remains of more pictures, some shreds of an oleograph, a suggestion of a steel engraving, some empty frames, the consumed remnants of another pope: 'Ah, the rats have them all ett,' she said firmly.

Turning to go, my eye was caught by something utterly frightful. Hanging in a row were some enormous furry creatures, bat-like, with their heads down, black and large as dogs. They hung in the half-light, four or five of them, their eyes glinting malevolently. Armed with the idea of discovering a hitherto unknown species of bat, *Genus Laloriensis*, I gained courage and approached what at the very least must be a coven of vampires. On inspection they turned out to be a row of ladies' fox furs which, having outlived fashion, survived here in a musty reliquary of clerics and quintuplets.

At the bottom of the stairs an obese spotted dog snarled from the kitchen threshold. After the sinister occupants of the upstairs rooms, he seemed decidedly friendly.

The Dark Edge of Europe

The Foothills of Mount Kidd

Ring Fort

Hilltop Farm

Isolated Farms

Path to the Spring

The Hills of Coomkeen

Gorse Fires & Mount Gabriel

La Bohème

Secluded Farm

The Upstairs Room

The Ancient of Days

Driscoll's Farm

INTERIORS

My little dribbly pen stretches
Across the great white paper plain,
Insatiable for splendid riches —
That is why my hand has pain.

ELEVENTH CENTURY AD

BEFORE THE ADVENT OF electricity life indoors was lived in semi-darkness. The more northerly the country the less light will penetrate the interior and if the windows are small, as they are in most traditional Irish rural dwellings, then the darkness can be perpetual and profound. The quality of light or dusk in one's living conditions exerts a considerable influence on the way one lives.

These *sfumato* conditions were commonplace on farms in West Cork up to fairly recent times. While oil-lamps and gas were available they lacked the spontaneousness of electric light and tended not to be used with the same freedom, and when electricity was installed people in the country found no compulsion to turn it on at the slightest darkening of the day. They were well accustomed to moving about easily in the twilight of their homes and in any case the traditional parsimony of 'sparing it' did not promote a dependence on things previously not needed. This familiarity with darkness seems to inspire a certain tranquility and without doubt encourages an unhurried pace of life. The homes, shops, pubs and churches of traditional communities all possessed this quality.

In the art of the past, particularly in any interior subject, there is a strong sense of how much life was governed by the seasons. Whether it is in the warm south or the cold north, Carravagio or Rembrandt, figures emerge from and disappear into the background as though it were part of them. Artists' ideas of light and shade, chiaroscuro, came from a direct observation of their own immediate world, not from a basis in theory. The problem with electricity is that it strips away all that sense of wholeness and leaves one instead with the microscopic vision, concentrating on the pores of the hand and forgetting the beauty of the form, the dexterity and grace of its movement.

In the interiors of Vermeer the viewer can see little evidence of action or even movement. Light enters in a shaft through a window; a woman reads a letter, stands by a musical instrument, or looks outside. The atmosphere is tranquil, unhurried; there is a sense of everything being in place, of comfortable well-being. Quite unlike Dutch genre painting of low life, where all is turmoil, noise and bustle, these paintings emanate quiet and a sense of timelessness. If you came back tomorrow things would be much the same. These are private worlds; the market-place is somewhere else, out of earshot.

When one finds in life the elements of art the experience is a startling one: the normal process of association is reversed. The familiar sensation of viewing a well-known painting, when encountered in reality, casts a double reflection which enhances both the original and its living image. I did not recognize my Vermeers for a long time after I had first encountered them. When eventually I did, I was so familiar with all the details of the canvas that recognition struck with considerable force. All the elements were there, even if the age, location and culture were different. Everything was in place and all the actors knew their parts perfectly. Even the light was right, a cold north-European one. My Vermeers were found in the homes of West Cork, in some of those light-dashed cottages on the hillside.

When you enter such a Vermeer the factor which distracts from instant recognition is that the ambience is not that of the merchant class but a peasant one. Amongst the few survivors of this society the value of an austere dignity has prevailed. The objects in the room are few and arranged with care. There are some shapes on the walls – pictures or a calendar – but the principal focus is on the space itself. The table by the window on which the necessary shaft of light falls is covered with a chequered cloth. Two or three household items are placed on this – a ceramic jug brimming with milk, a steel-bladed knife with a timber handle, a folded newspaper – refracting the light. These few things define the normal affairs of the occupants. The human presence is minimal: a woman standing or sitting by the window, engaged in some slow, domestic task; a man sitting in a shadowed corner. All conversation is superfluous, while the silences are real communication, interspersed with the occasional question and answer or an exchange of civilities.

It is in the tenebrous atmosphere of the small, old-fashioned pub interiors that the tranquility of darkness most completely survives. The screen at the window, decorated on the outside with advertisements for brands of whiskey and stout which ceased production before the First World War, obscures all but the echo of street life outside. Behind the bar counter the proprietor is seated in a corner ruminating, or perhaps squinting at the small ads columns of the local newspaper, the print barely visible in the faint light. Outside the counter a solitary farmer sits on a stool with a half-consumed glass in front of him. The only sound to break into his reverie is the rustle of the paper. An hour passes and the farmer appears not to have moved nor his drink visibly diminished, while the woman behind the counter continues to scrutinize the small print.

With a slight sound the street door opens. Another man enters and seats himself at the counter. Noiselessly the owner moves down the length of narrow space between the shelves of drinks and the high counter. A mutter of voices and a drink is placed before the man. He consumes it hurriedly, places a few coins on the counter and with a nod leaves by the back entrance. The newspaper is taken up again in the corner and the man on the stool seems rooted to the spot, immobile, though the level in his glass has dropped slightly. Somewhere in a back room an old-fashioned wall clock sounds the hour with an ancient and asthmatic chime and the sound hangs in the air long after the hour has been struck. Without preamble the woman behind the bar looks over her glasses at the man and says, 'The hay is very dear'. He raises his head, pauses, and replies: 'It is'.

This tranquility of mind is bred of stoicism in the face of insuperable odds: the land, the weather, personal demons and political unrest. Climate and environment have a considerable influence on the development of those regional characteristics most visible to the outsider, qualities accepted as the norm by those who know no other. Eschewing the frivolous and ephemeral, the inhabitants of the half-light dwell on their words and use them sparingly. They have some of that spirit of renunciation which is captured in the terse personal comments left by the monks of the little monasteries in the margins of their manuscripts. They also knew this land and its silences.

I painted a series of watercolours of these austerely beautiful interior subjects some years ago, but only after an understanding of their Vermeer-like essence had struck me. In doing these paintings I looked further into both the form and content of this austerity and saw in it one of the greatest hurdles to be overcome in appreciating the stoic virtues of the rural Irish environment: the merits of its landscape and architecture can hardly be understood when what is simple is construed as representing only poverty and deprivation.

Church of St Brendan the Navigator, Crookhaven

The Island

Interior with Icon

Frugal Interiors

Winter Light

'The Rocks of Bawn'

A Quiet Pint

THE ERSATZ SHOP

'What falsehood would suit the occasion best?' she asked herself hurriedly.

GEORGE MOORE **A Drama in Muslin**

THE TINY SHOPS WHOSE facades still line the main streets of many West Cork villages and towns have the proportions of living-rooms. Many have become just that while others have been absorbed into larger establishments and disappeared without trace. Yet some have survived, preserving an intimate atmosphere of personal service and domestic life.

The door-bell rings at your entry and the shopkeeper comes out from the family's kitchen or parlour behind the shop. The shop-space is minute and so its stock surrounds you on all levels, mounting to the ceiling in shoe-boxes and odd containers of brown paper and string. It is in these little stores that you find the precursor of the supermarket idea, in which all human needs are kept under one roof. String and bicycle pumps, bathing caps for ladies next to packages of detergent, penny sweets and salted fish, a pig's head on a large platter, batteries for your transistor radio, homemade cakes and caustic soda. Farmers' wives (the shop can only accommodate three customers) are buying their weekly supplies of groceries and, in defiance of EC strictures, delivering farm eggs or homemade butter. Exchange and barter are still viable in these intimate surroundings. You have come in search of something quite ordinary, an innocuous purchase – sultanas or baking powder perhaps. The woman behind the counter, hemmed in on all sides by boxes and jars, prepares your package and accepts the money. You are asked a question concerning your purchase or the weather, your mother's health or how the cousin who visited you several years ago and now living in New Zealand is faring. Your change remains firmly grasped in your interrogant's hand as the enquiry continues. When you have parted with the requisite amount of news you receive your purchase. That is the real business of the day; the pound of onions merely a token. In the days when these tiny shops functioned up and down the main street, shopping in a village must have had an atmosphere resembling the intimacy and secrecy of the confessional. A pound of tea from Minehan's: you slip in, the question is asked, the token exchanged; you emerge and proceed to the next cubicle.

Naturally not all shops served the same purpose. Most were general groceries in the widest sense of the term, the rest most probably pubs.

Some belonged to an exclusive category of village curiosity: the ersatz shop. This species of emporium, peculiar to Irish towns and villages, has so many representatives that they make up an important cultural sub-genre. What one can never decide is: has the ersatz shop failed in business or never actually begun to trade? Its front door will be expectantly open; behind the window to the kitchen a head passes, definite evidence of life on the premises; but there is nothing, or rather, practically nothing for sale. On the counter a basket contains two loaves of bread, the shop's only concession to freshness; the shelves are sparsely decorated with single items: one tin of beans, one package of bread soda. Two boxes of grey chocolate bars in faded wrapping betray a sudden, extravagant impulse of overstocking. All the items on the vacant shelves have the air of a still life about them, as though the package of tea and the jar of Marmite have been carefully arranged for maximum effect. The place looks like a stage set of the minimalist school. The emphasis is on suggestion. In the ersatz shop decorum requires one to request an item visibly not in stock in order not to disturb the display. A response which I have frequently encountered, not just in these establishments but also in those apparently thriving, is, 'They don't make that any more', even though the product in question is probably on display in every other shop in the village.

The external architecture of the village shop is a case of variations on a theme. Two traditions, those of the eighteenth and nineteenth centuries, appear to co-exist. The earlier style is of a rigorous absence of decoration. The window, divided by thin glazing bars, is flanked by simple strip pilasters and above it the fascia which carries the name is covered by a severe cornice. The door adjoining the window and tucked under the fascia is solid, or has a minute glazed panel. The older the shop the smaller the panes in the window. Some are like pigeon holes, rows of little panes, and now few such survive as they are anathema to the principles of modern window display. The later or more Baroque style in shop facades has many delightful features, less dumpy proportions, and makes no concession to the 'old curiosity shop' image. Here all is redolent of wealthy Victorian merchants, proud of their wares and their prosperity. The most notable feature is a flowering of the pilasters into decorated columns topped by console brackets, the latter rearing out above the pavement like a pair of figureheads on the prow of a sailing ship. Although uncommon, bare-breasted female figures are occasionally to be found in this position. Decoration on the Victorian shop-front runs to all sorts of fancies: brass or cast-iron bars suitable for *en point* in a ballet studio prevent loungers from leaning against the plate glass; enamel, gilding, mirrors, engraved glass, arched panes and marbling all combine to enrich the premises and advertize the worth of both merchant and merchandize. The interiors tend to reflect the external style and while the small plain shops have deal counters and box shelving their grander neighbours go to excessive lengths of extravagance with mahogany, ceramic fittings and veritable orgies of mirrors.

Modern taste naturally tends towards other things and the prosperity of the last twenty years has cast much of the decor and the facades onto the scrap-heap. Fortunately, before the rout was total, a swing back towards the more craftsman-like ideas of the past became apparent; indeed, centred in the town of Clonakilty, a minor revolution is taking place in the shop-fronts of the whole countryside. There had existed in West Cork a strong tradition of decorative signwriting, firmly based on nineteenth-century typographical styles. The traditional signwriters of the area evolved a strong and dignified style capable of enhancing even the most dismal premises. Allied to a sense of the visual effect of words and an understanding of their power as a medium, they had a love of extinct terms and archaic phrases: Victuallers, Haberdashery, Medical Hall – rich and evocative words. Then came the era of the plastic sign and a fine, decorative art form went into premature decline, and the richness of language which had been an integral part of the calligraphic tradition disappeared also. Gaelic scripts, broadsheet bold lettering, Roman, sculptural, majuscule and miniscule, all succumbed to the monotony and flatness of plastic illiteracy. The doldrums prevailed for a generation and then, suddenly, living calligraphy began to appear again. Now it has attained an influence so strong as to force the plastic off the streets; the traditional shop-front, or a modern interpretation of it, has supplanted the latter-day colonialism of plastic, formica and beauty-board. The renaissance is being carried by artist-craftsmen imbued with a deep love of their skill and consciously contributing to the visual culture of the entire population.

Sometimes a particular sign catches the eye; it attracts, irritates, confuses or baffles one. A bed-and-breakfast placard under the apparently Serbo-Croat or perhaps Coptic name, NINORC, certainly puzzled me. Could it be a townland, the family name, some conjunction of personal names? I could not work it out. In the etching process the picture is drawn in reverse on a wax-covered sheet of metal and printed in mirror image. When I was working on the etching plate of the Skibbereen carpenter's, P. Cronin, I reversed my drawing to prepare the image. The enigmatic NINORC appeared before my eyes, a puzzle solved.

The names of the family owners appear over the doors of most businesses. Cronin's, Sheehan's, O'Toole's, designate the shop or pub. Almost anything might be lurking behind the opaque facade of a pub; its door may be the back entrance to the betting office for all you know. The interiors are linked, male-dominated enclaves of secret conversations and strange transactions. The entrance to the betting office is like that of a beehive. All day the patrons dart in and out of the oblique opening. The observer cannot see what is happening inside. Suddenly there is a flurry of activity and just as rapidly it dies away. Men emerge scrutinizing small slips of paper and drift off down the street. Like the pub it is a closed world to the uninitiated.

The pub may honestly announce its presence with signs and its characteristic blind aspect – those windows designed neither for looking in nor for looking out – or be tucked away behind what to the public looks like a bicycle shop or a dry-goods merchant. Of all the crossovers from one branch of business to another these are without doubt the most charming. Instead of drink being sold in exclusively alcohol-orientated surroundings, here you drink your pint amongst galvanized buckets and farm implements. Then there is the institution of the snug. A fast-vanishing aspect of Irish drinking practice, this is a cubicle screened off from the rest of the bar where conversation will not be disturbed nor the drinkers observed. Comfort is eschewed in favour of absolute privacy: the bench is hard, there is barely space for one's knees, and the concealing partition is high. Somewhere in the wall a Judas window opens and a disembodied hand appears with your order. A discreet knock on this sliding panel will bring fresh supplies.

Listening to an old man in a bar one day, I gleaned from him the idea of developing a defence against small-shop interrogation. A big farmer had been talking at length of his prodigious experience at trapping badgers. The old man listened, adding, at appropriate intervals, 'You did so', or, 'I know it well myself', to encourage the talker to greater lengths. When the farmer had expended his store of wisdom and anecdote on the trapping and killing of the inoffensive poor badger, he finished his pint and left. The door closed with a little click and there was silence for a while as the few occupants of the pub dwelt on what they had heard or ruminated about other matters. With a slight cough the old man alerted people's attention. He turned around to face me with a smile and pronounced his verdict.

'There's nothing I like,' said he, 'like a good lie.'

What better answer could there be to unwanted queries than an unacceptable reply?

'And how is that cousin who was visiting you this time twelve months?'

'Oh, locked up long ago.'

Country post offices provide an excellent subject for anthropological, let alone architectural, study and, what's more, test one's wits. They vary considerably not just in size but also in the very concept of what is implied by their title. The sale of stamps and related material, and the care of the mails, would probably cover the normal areas of interest. But in the country it obviously means much more than that and can cover everything from general store to community centre. My personal taste is for those post offices of an older and more austere spirit where commerce has not totally swamped the true core of their activity. Imagine my joy one day on walking into a tiny village post office and seeing the young man behind the counter wearing earphones and tapping out a message. This was an example of just the sort of contempt for progress that I find charming, as long as I am not trying to make a long-distance call. However, it was not so. The postmistress was at lunch and her young son was minding the shop, wearing his personal stereo and tapping in time to the music. But another pleasurable encounter with the past, and this time no illusion, was to walk into an unfamiliar village and find the last of a genre, a post office with a 'No Spitting' sign. The space was as bare as the interior of the great pyramid, with dust on everything and no concessions to the modern world in evidence.

'Have you any postcards?' I asked.

'Ah, there's no call for them,' came the firm reply.

My local post office has long ago left the ranks of bare boards and admonitions against expectoration. Resembling more the style of the bar-grocery, the relevant service is contained in a corner cubicle, somewhat hidden from the customer. The mystic rites of the sub-postmistress are not, apparently, for the eyes of lesser mortals. Surrounding the aperture in her cubicle is evidence of a fairly successful camouflage artist at work: on the counter, where you hope to lay your money, an arrangement of massed toilet rolls gives the impression of a defensive embankment while suspended displays of mass-cards and calenders provide convincing foliage effects. Behind all this the sale of stamps proceeds; there is a firm sensation of dealing in contraband or sacred relics. When the number of customers can be counted on two fingers of one hand the pendulous lid of the aperture falls, no doubt to preserve the sanctity of the transaction. To succeed in handing in your money and receive your stamps is on a par with the chances of the sun's rays penetrating the interior of the great tumulus at Newgrange – only possible on the solstice and even then dependent on the weather.

Adèle's, Schull

Tig na nGaedhal, Skibbereen

Saddler, Bantry

Hayes Bar, Union Hall

Barber's Shop, Skibbereen

Gentleman's Hairdressing, Bantry

The Winning Post, Bantry

North Street, Skibbereen

Bar-Hardware, Bantry

The Bridges of Skibbereen

Main Street, Clonakilty

'Ninorc'

THE SPEAKING STONES

The *rath* survives; the kings
are covered in clay.

SIXTH CENTURY AD

WHEN WE WERE BOYS my brother and I spent much of the long summer months cycling around the roads of north County Cork in search of antiquities and specimens for our private museum. This institution was installed in a room in our house and was composed of bizarre junk, natural history and historical flotsam. Fossils and coins, birds' eggs, butterflies and moths, stamps and minerals, antique radios and telephones, militaria, antlers, clothes for dressing up and some extraordinary Polynesian ceremonial regalia. With the extensive brief we set ourselves virtually anything could be, and was, included.

During our expeditions we evolved a dictum of such an infallible nature that I offer it to all professional antiquarians concerned with the study of castles, monastic ruins and – our firm favourite – fortified mansions. This principle was developed so as to discern whether a ruin, when seen from a distance, had its floors or stairs intact. To a middle-aged scholar it may seem unimportant whether or not a castle has floors in comparison to whether or not it withstood the siege of 1641 or was sacked by the terrible O'Driscolls, but from the point of view of twelve- and thirteen-year-old antiquarians the matter is of the utmost urgency. If there are no floors or only fragments of stairs one cannot climb to the top, and what is the point of a castle if it can only be admired from below? Lalor's Law of Castles, expounded in those years, stated that, 'If you can't see the sky through the castle from the ground when a quarter of a mile away, then it has floors'. This observation saved a lot of last-minute dashes to be the first one to the top.

With few exceptions, the castles of the coastal region of West Cork and the Mizen peninsula fail to qualify under Lalor's Law. A second law might also be expounded to save the weary tourist from emerging from the car to face farm dogs of xenophobic zeal or fields of mad cattle who, in rude defiance of the norms of nature, stampede towards rather than away from the timid stranger. Lalor's Second Law of Castles states that, 'Castles standing on a rocky promontory are a dead loss as the side you can't see has fallen into the sea'. This condition leaves a kind of Wild West shop-front effect so that, for example, when one gets nearer the last stronghold of the O'Mahonys, the stronghold turns out to be a mere wall with an amazed bullock lodged half-way up on a ledge. And as the antiquarian tourist will most probably be a fellow-traveller of the RSPCA the plight of the trapped bullock must be reported to the nearest farmhouse. A conversation then follows so chilling to any lover of old stones that you wish the bovine climber and his master to be cast together into the sea.

In nineteenth-century copies of *Punch* the Irish cartoons generally depicted a dialogue between a noble-visaged, tweed-clad gentleman called Saxon tourist, and a simian, witless creature called Pat. Such caricatures can still be employed.

Saxon tourist: 'There is a bullock stuck half-way up the wall of the castle. It may fall and be killed if it is not rescued.'

Pat: 'Is it me you're telling? She won't go up again when I have that old rubbish knocked down for my new road.'

While local awareness of the importance of old sites is growing rapidly, and the farmer you encounter now may in fact be the president of the local historical society, the development of modern earth-moving equipment has made great destruction possible. What would in the past have taken twenty men a month to accomplish may now be performed by one man with a bulldozer in a matter of days. Recent surveys of the West Cork area show that since the original Ordnance Survey records of 1837 more than a third of all antiquities noted then have disappeared. The bulldozer is not the sole aggressor. Wars and weather have denuded practically all the castles in the country of their roofs, and West Cork is no exception. Indeed, the child antiquarian failed to form an observation on this subject as he had never encountered a roofed ruin.

The best preserved and the most beautifully sited of the West Cork castles is Kilcoe which sits on a rood of rock, Mannin Beg, overlooking Roaring Water Bay from its eastern side. Built, like most of these castles, in the late sixteenth century, Kilcoe passes Lalor's Law with flying colours: you cannot see through it from any point and consequently there is an abundance of floors and stairs. A stronghold of the McCarthys, its elaborate construction and substantial fortifications enabled it to resist siege by the English for two years after the battle of Kinsale. Its separation from the mainland by a sea-channel must have helped it later to survive pillage by landowners; opposite it, on the far shore, is White Castle, cannibalized in the late eighteenth century to provide stone for the adjoining manor house. Only the stub of that tower remains.

Art is a dangerous business, not to be embraced by the faint of heart. Kilcoe twice made an attempt on the life of this artist, albeit passively. The first occasion was when I had come to live nearby in 1974 and was exploring the castle for the first time. Having studied it outside and in, observed some carved stone heads decorating an upper window and been exhilirated by the view from the top, I returned to ground level and skirted the outside. I noticed that by climbing up inside a damaged portion of the wall one could enter a secondary tower, inaccessible from the main stucture. Scrambling inside without difficulty I found myself at the base of a succession of small rooms. The lowest of these had an opening in the floor, no doubt the entrance to a dungeon.

This exciting discovery had to be investigated. Shining my torch into the space below revealed nothing as it belled out like an old ink-bottle and echoed with a dark, hollow sense of being limitless and bottom-less. I found a large spar and lowered it into the empty space until it touched the floor some twenty feet below. On this angled spar of wood I slid down into Fergus McCarthy's dungeon. Sliding down was easy: reality struck the moment my feet touched on the floor of mud and rough stones. Looking up, Wilde's 'little tent of blue which prisoners call the sky' alerted me to my predicament. Now caricature characters exchanged roles: I remembered my torch resting safely above at the mouth of the dungeon.

Pat: 'What are you doing down there your honour?'

Saxon tourist: 'I am looking up at you making a spectacle of yourself!'

Panic set in at once: the smooth spar was unclimbable. When I moved away from it my feet touched water. For the first time in this enterprise I began to think. Had I told my wife, at home with our young child, where I was going? How many days would it take before someone would find and identify my bicycle, lying in a nearby fuchsia hedge? Would a search party ever find its way to this hidden place?

I may have left my torch above but at least I had carried my shoulder-bag with me. The condemned man ate a hearty meal – well, a sandwich and an apple – while he contemplated fellow sufferers of incarceration. Somehow the little prince in the tower was not an apt parallel; the grisly illustrations to *The Pit and the Pendulum* by Harry Clarke were more appropriate. As the damp began to penetrate my bones a vague recollection of Vercingetorix dying in a cistern in ancient Rome seemed quite perfect.

Time passed. I made more efforts to climb the spar but only managed a few feet before sliding down again. Later, with welts on my hands and a feeling of dread in my heart, I began to crave something to eat. There wasn't even a crumb in my bag but, in searching, my fingers touched something smooth and cold. Nails, by God. I was saved! A dozen good-sized masonry nails lay glinting in my palm in the dark. With a stone I hammered them at intervals into the wood and, ascending, hammered in some more until I was again safely on the castle floor. My Lazarus-like emergence from the chill of the tomb had a chastening effect on my spirit of adventure after that, but years later Kilcoe was to make a further attempt on my person. In broad daylight too.

In the etchings and engravings of Dürer and his contemporaries the landscape backgrounds have an abundance of fine realistic detail. The viewpoint is often high, with a town by a lake or a castle on a crag indicating the small human presence in the midst of rude nature. It is a landscape of untamed beauty with each change of terrain accentuated, The landscape of West Cork has retained much of this sense of detail, with the small efforts of man being surrounded by the greater efforts of time, chance and change. Lacking the boundless fields of twentieth-century agriculture and the vast roads which always accompany such expanses, the local landscape is one of small fields, clusters of buildings in tight groupings, castles on crags and an infinite membrane of winding and narrow roads. The high viewpoint favoured by the artists of Dürer's time has always interested me and I have used this angle of vision frequently in my work, both in real and imaginary contexts.

In my etchings the interior of Kilcoe Castle shows the main living chamber, with the external form of the building indicated in the distance through the window. I went to the castle many years after my incarceration in Fergus McCarthy's dungeons, and on a bright and cloudless day in May, with the waters of Roaring Water Bay sparkling around me, I mounted the steep stairs to the main apartment of the building. Although roofless this room is still spacious and elegant, with four deeply-set window embrasures facing the cardinal points. The one shown in my etching is the best preserved and faces west. One has fallen out, leaving a jagged hole in the wall; another is intact, but the sill and floor have collapsed leaving a space open to the sky.

Sitting on some fallen masonry I paused periodically to rest my eyes from the intense light of the day and the effort of concentration, observing details and assessing proportions. Occasionally I got up and wandered around the room, trying to imagine the people that it had once sheltered and how abruptly a century of life here was snuffed out. In an anonymous ballad of the last century its final days were described in heroic words.

> Now, Fergus, now your soldiers call! this
> night decides your fate,
> Place twenty men upon the wall and
> twenty at the gate;
> For underneath we see the plumes of the
> accursed foe,
> Who come to rack and gut and sack this
> castle of Kilcoe.

These verses give victory to the besieged, history awards it to the accursed foe, while fate brought the castle to the purchase of a genuine Saxon tourist in the 1960s as a holiday home. Fortunately, it still remains a ruin.

Returning to my perch I continued to draw until I was finished, and then stood up and walked across to one of the windows, my eyes fixed on the distant view framed by the stone mullions. I paused momentarily, and found myself to be standing on the loose bottom stones of the missing sill with only air around me and a long, long drop to the rocks and sea below. I froze, willing my body to reverse its momentum outward into the empty space of seagulls and sky. It was not the day for Icarus and I managed to regain the *terra firma* of the room, drained by my unconsciously suicidal walk. The drawing was still in my hands. I lay on the floor for a long time and absorbed the flying clouds overhead. When I take the copperplate of the etching in my hands to print it now, I have an overpowering sense of vertigo.

* * * * *

Echoes of war at Kilcoe yield to recollections of silent contemplation at Gougane Barra where, to the east of Bantry Bay, the island hermitage of Saint Finbarr projects into a lake surrounded by precipitous hills. Approached from the village of Inchigeela, the distinguishing feature of the island is the steeply pitched roof of the minute chapel. This structure, built in the Romanesque Revival style, is in fact a fairly dull and spiritless attempt to simulate the architecture of the saint's time, though it does echo what may have existed here, like the buildings of Glendalough, in the smallness of its scale.

Hidden amidst a mass of trees is a curious rectangular enclosure. A series of steps leads up into a courtyard surrounded by deep recesses, each with a narrow ledge at the rear. In the centre a wooden cross stands on a stepped platform. This is Saint Finbarr's oratory, eighteenth-century style, a pastiche closely related to the folly and the cottage orné, which was perpetrated by the Reverend Dennis O'Mahony who later abandoned the world to live as a hermit in his windy and fanciful creation. The hermits would have to have been not only severe ascetics but also accomplished yogi to have been able to sleep on the ledges provided in their apartments. The wooden cross which dominates the centre of the enclosure has had countless pennies hammered into its surface by the penitents who have come here on pilgrimage. One wonders at the significance of such violent gestures in a place of pilgrimage.

Overlooking the road and causeway to the island is a small graveyard of tottering stones enclosed by a wall of ragged masonry, and below the wall a gated archway closely resembling the hermits' bedsits on the opposite shore. Amongst the usual inscriptions commemorating vigorous procreation and abject piety is one to a noted local storyteller, Tadhg Ó Buachalla, whose sharp wit and pithy conversation have been recorded in *The Tailor and Ansty*. The inscription is a startling assertion of self, at marked variance with the anonymity of its neighbours and suggestive of a happier view of life than that implied in the defacing of a wooden cross and the nation's currency simultaneously. It reads: *A star danced and under that I was born.*

The island hermitage and Kilcoe Castle each offer particular voices in stone and speak in accents both of functional concerns of defense and accommodation and motivating concerns of religion and politics. In 1984 I decided to turn my attention to surviving examples of the use of stone by artists in the area. Excluding the Big House from my brief I concentrated on those aspects of art which might be expected to survive in public places such as churches and churchyards, town squares and ruins. By excluding the art collections of Big Houses I was left with functional art, commemorative and memorial art and works of recent and remote antiquity. In previous excursions I had seen much which might reward a second look; now I was determined to cast my net as widely as possible and to include all manner of things. No sculptures by Michelangelo or frescoes by Rubens were either expected or encountered, but if we cannot have eagles we may as well be pigeon fanciers.

Pigeons there were in plenty, ranging from a school of republican sculptors working in a style last popular in the Egypt of the Pharaohs, to such wonders as the sixth Baron Carberry carved in a larger than life-size marble statue and portrayed in Elizabethan fancy dress, apparently on his way to the ball. Seriousness of intent seems to have misfired in both these cases to produce results both comic and grotesque. The baron, aptly named Lord Freke, now resting in the outer nave of Roscarberry Cathedral, is the work of a highly respected though evidently humourless Dutch sculptor, William Geefs. It is a rather chilling and sobering thought that this piece of absurd and splendidly rendered frivolity was carved while the Famine was devastating the population of the surrounding area. Although an improving landlord, Baron Carberry's doublet and hose do not give the impression of a man in touch with his time. In the same vein of aristocratic effigies is the tomb of the second Earl of Bandon in St Peter's church, Bandon. This wholly successful recumbent figure by the English sculptor, Richardson, achieves precisely what was intended; that is, to impress one with the dignity and worthiness of this Victorian nobleman, laid out in his robes with every button and braid carved in the most minute detail.

After the establishment of the Irish Free State monuments were erected all over the country to commemorate the revolutionary leaders. These memorials contributed a category of naive art to the body of public statuary which had previously been the work of professional sculptors. Most of these works were not commissioned from sculptors, the job being given instead to the local funerary mason, as is evident from the results. The statue of Sean Hales in Bandon is a relevant example. With the stiffness of an attendant at the side of a Pharaoh, Sean Hales stands on top of his pedestal suggesting a tin soldier rather than a revolutionary hero. The mason must have worked from a photograph of his subject in just such a pose, arms glued to his sides, spine ramrod straight, eyes staring into the future. What the statue does capture quite well is some breath of the sterile vision of these post-revolutionary times. Another even more remote hero is the figure of O'Donovan Rossa at the entrance to Rossa Park in Skibbereen. In this case the style tends more towards South American socialist-realism, probably an unconscious empathy on the part of the artist. O'Donovan Rossa, like Sean Hales and all the other heroes standing aloft in market squares and crossroads, fixes his eyes on the distant horizon. A body is there, only the spirit is missing.

Little evidence is to be found amongst the peers, lords, bishops and heroes of the delightful, the charming, the human. This was not the way they wished posterity to see them, or, more likely, not the way they saw themselves. You have to go back to the old Gaelic or Anglo-Norman society to find anything that hints at the personal, at least among the remains which I came across. About a half-mile off the main road near Dunmanway is the castle of Ballynacarriga. In two window embrasures in the main chamber on the upper floor are carvings in low relief commemorating the family which lived there in the sixteenth century. What is so singular about these modest carvings is that they contain the earliest portrait of a West Cork person, and that it should be of a woman, Catherine Cullinane, wife of Randall Hurley. She is shown in Elizabethan dress; three roses represent her three children, while her initials and those of her husband are also carved. The castle, a tower house like Kilcoe, can hardly have been comfortable, yet one has the feeling that these were civilized people, living in troubled times.

The castle of Ballynacarriga – the townland of stones – is at one with the all-pervasive stoniness of the area. Stones formed the character of the land as the earliest inhabitants must have found it, and it was with stone that they left their permanent signs on the landscape. On the slopes of Mount Kidd a byway meanders towards the brow of the land, skirting the steeper sides of the mountain; hidden by the blackthorns which line the road is a stone surface inscribed with markings executed over four thousand years ago. These strange lines and circles, gouged into the bedrock of the land, contain an intelligence as opaque as the art of Newgrange. From this first expression of who knows what astronomical, ritualistic or cultic wisdom the use of stone grew commonplace; standing stones, dolmens, stone circles, continued the ritual in rock. In a later age these things were invested with an aura of superstition, the last glimmering of the respect with which they were once held in more ancient societies.

On an awkward spine of rocky land outside Castletownshend stands a stone alignment known variously as 'The Five Fingers' or 'Fionn MacCumhail's Fingers'. Raised high above the road the finger-like stones rise out of the land in the form of a hand outstretched; this setting is the work of a considerable sensibility and must have been all the more imposing when the landscape was not circumscribed by field-fences and roadways. In the last century one of the ladies of Castletownshend had a monolith carried off from this arrangement to decorate her garden, an oblique if unfortunate tribute to the anonymous master who placed them there.

A close cousin of these standing stones, though separated from them by a wide expanse of time, is the Kilnaruane Pillar Stone, also sited on a high place overlooking the town of Bantry and its bay. A simple stone pillar from the early Christian period, it too displays an innate sense of appropriateness as to location and decoration. Two sides of this rectangular pillar are carved in low relief with decorations that might excite a contemporary sculptor by their simplicity, symbolism and humour. Within the panels of Celtic interlace are arranged little pictures of local life representing religious themes. Sailing vertically up one surface is a currach with people in it, presumed to represent St Brendan's voyage. On the other side stands the figure of an ecclesiastic with arms raised in prayer; below him two figures sit at a table as a bird brings them bread, a scene interpreted as St Paul and St Anthony in the desert being given bread by a crow. Rural themes and fantastic legends entwine to decorate a memorial to some now unknown inhabitant of this land.

On my desk papers are kept in place by a seashore stone, of a size to fit comfortably in the hand, which I found high up on the side of Mount Gabriel. What was it doing there, so far from the sea? This stone, which is blackened on one side, is a maul from the Bronze Age mines which were operated on the mountainside and which remain undisturbed even today, left more or less as the miners abandoned them. Using fire and water to shatter the rock and mauls to crush the ore-bearing fragments, these pioneer industrialists provided the copper which was mixed with Cornish tin to become the raw material of Ireland's Heroic Age. Those fingers may not have been Fionn Mac-Cumhail's, but undoubtedly the hands which held my maul were well versed in the character and quality of the stones of this landscape.

Kilcoe Castle, Roaring Water Bay

Kilcoe

O'Driscoll's Castle, Baltimore

Gougane Barra

1798 Monument, Clonakilty

Stone Circle & Child Sacrifice

The Kilnaruane Pillar Stone, Bantry

TOWNS AND VILLAGES

'The child works sixteen hours a day and feeds like
the Irish, on potatoes fried in rat's dripping.'

Honoré de Balzac **Cousin Bette**, 1846

I WAS STANDING ON the main street of Bantry, one could say minding my own business. I was drawing some feature of the town and being jostled by the crowds. It was Fair Day and my timing might have been better. Frantic crowds of shoppers do not provide the ideal circumstances for executing anything with much precision. A good moment for observation, certainly, but being assaulted by men carrying sacks of carrots or others aggressively wielding limp houseplants is hardly very conducive to maintaining one's concentration. When my glasses were nearly knocked off by a passing head of cabbage my equanimity began to wear slightly thin. Then an obsequious drunk parked his reeking person next to mine and wished to discuss my activity in between cadging the price of a drink. I got rid of him with some pointed rudeness and continued to draw, to be joined a few minutes later by a simpleton who stood so close to me that drawing had to be suspended while I dealt with this rather difficult diversion. Not wishing to be hurtful I sent this admirer off into the crowd to follow a man, hoping not to see either again. All this was not improving my temper and by now the drawing looked like something produced by a clever chimpanzee. I was getting hot and irritable and sense should have recommended a quiet pint in a secluded snug, leaving creativity for some more propitious occasion. Nothing of the sort occurred to me then, of course: I was determined to finish my work and wished the citizens of Bantry to hell or much preferably to Connaught, the latter being further away as it turned out.

A shadow fell on my drawing pad and I glanced up in annoyance, expecting further harrassment. I was right. Two large men in ill-fitting business suits were shaking collection boxes at me and obscuring my last remnant of a view. What could they possibly want? They quickly answered my unspoken question. 'Help the boys on the blanket,' the larger one said, in tones more righteous than obsequious. It was 1981, the era of the hunger strikers, and these missionaries from the North were evidently not having a good day for it was hot and the crowd, intent on bargains, was indifferent.

The venom which I had accumulated for the cabbage-wielding

fairgoers found a target. Looking over my now ruined drawing I said to them, 'Capped any good knees lately?'

Their composure snapped instantly and I found myself grabbed from both sides by large hands. With a twist I got free and, now thankful for the crowd, I dashed off, pursued by my assailants. I slipped into a pub which I knew had a rear exit. Out the back was a narrow alleyway, and this led me up past the smithy some distance away. I returned to my car by a circuitous route, shaking with dismay at my unwise sally.

I never quite hit if off with Bantry, somehow. Some years later a commission came my way to do a series of perspective drawings of a proposed museum which would commemorate the ill-fated French fleet which had come to grief in the bay in 1796. The drawings were produced and the representative of the committee was pleased. Later, they asked me if I would like to design the project (having been an architect in a previous life) and I gladly agreed. After some considerable time-lapse a meeting was arranged for all the relevant people representing those organizations with irons in this particular fire. It took place in the library of Bantry House, in the grounds of which the museum was to be located. It was an impressive gathering, if polished shoe-leather and well-sharpened pencils are any criteria. I was not in possession of either of these assets. Indeed, when the assembled shiny-shoes drew their pencils and set to work on the plan, I began to wonder if I were in the right place. The question was the position of the stairs and in a little while the relatively small building resembled a storeroom for redundant staircases, with six alternatives in happy co-existence. As I did not possess a pencil, and certainly not a rapier-sharp one, it would have seemed churlish to have added my considered opinion with a biro. The fate of the French fleet, overburdened with enthusiasm yet less than welcome, struck me as an appropriate motif for my involvement in the scheme. My demise followed fairly swiftly afterwards. In architecture, as in art, one needs a sense of perspective.

Unlike the phenonemon of proliferating staircases, the common-place arrangement of Irish villages is a case of growth rather than planning. The development is that of the node on the stem: a main street, usually so called, pushes out offshoots, each of which is given a precise topographical description – High Street, Pier Road, and so on. The road has come from somewhere and has somewhere to go; the houses of the village merely form an interlude, and line the road with the curiosity of an idle crowd awaiting a procession.

To this invariable rule Castletownshend is an exception. The houses certainly follow the main street but this descends a steep hill and ends abruptly in the sea. Half-way down the main street is the Eros of the place, an absurd stonebuilt enclosure from which two gangling sycamores obstruct any further view of the street. In a dream of delusion the local council, perhaps imagining Picaddily-like traffic conditions, announced this Eros to be a traffic hazard. In Castletown-shend, traffic must be considered in the singular. People protested and the council relented.

The village's only offshoot is called the Mall and it is lined with patrician houses half-hidden by high walls. A lumpen Gothick castle languishes behind stern gates at the bottom of the main street and above it stands the church on a rocky crag. This is Saint Barrahane's, Church of Ireland. The Catholic church was sited a mile outside the village where its Romish airs would not impinge on the rational Anglican manners of the citadel. The Ó Buachalla inscription in Gougane Barra, with its pantheist fancy, finds an echo in Saint Barrahane's in what are the most splendid stained-glass windows to be seen on the whole Mizen peninsula. Hidden in a recess in the altar apse is a small, gem-like window done by Harry Clarke around 1926 and reeking of *fin de siècle* decadence. The elongated figures with their ethereal expressions imply an intensity of emotion not normally found in portrayals of Irish saints. The window shows St Luke, patron saint of artist, who is reputed to have painted the Virgin.

Castletownshend is the hub of the Somerville and Ross Lake District. Edith Somerville lived most of her long and productive life in the village, alternately writer, artist, horse-dealer, master of fox-hounds, occultist and organist. The tone of the *ancien regime* is quieter now, its monuments still dignified but abandoned by the culture which gave them life. The tenor is diluted by a leaven of tourists, happy to have bed-and-breakfast in the castle and attend summer schools in the big house. In the future Castletownshend will echo with the memories of a vanished race, dislodged by a quirk of history.

Sitting quietly with some friends over a pint in the sunlight of a pub yard off the main street, I stretched idly up to a blossom-laden branch and plucked one. From above came a rattle of windows and before a face could be seen a voice roared in commanding tones, honed on ranks of sepoys and elderly tea-wallahs in Chittagong: 'What the devil do you think you're doing? This is not a public park, y'know'. The sort of face sported by Bertie Wooster's aunts, for it was a woman not a man, glared from a window above. Strong features, apoplectic eyes, wild white hair. No reply was offered, nor was one expected, as the sepoys stared into their pints. The old order changeth, but slowly.

A rather pointed but hardly very poignant reminder of the time when society really did know where everyone stood is recorded in the organ loft of Saint Barrahane's. Lining the nave are the marble armorials of the first families of the citadel; up in the loft, and doubtless nearer to God, were the servants. A plaque, tiny in comparison with the vast family histories displayed below, shows how securely God was in his heaven and all was right with the world.

This Gallery erected July 1828
was the gift of
HENRIETTA TOWNSEND
of Castle Townsend For the
accommodation of the lower orders
of the Tenantry of Castle Townsend
Estate and for the use of such
other poor persons in the Parish
of Castle Haven as may require
accommodation The gallery to
remain forever for these
exclusive purposes

From their loft the lower orders must have had a fine view of the flowered hats and pomaded hair of those on whom God had so satisfactorily smiled. The lastmentioned provision of Henrietta Townsend's inscription has, of course, been ignored and the gallery now accommodates the organ. The name of her village has been tampered with too: an 'h' was introduced later on in the nineteenth century to make it sound 'more aristocratic', or so the promoters of this change considered.

Evidence of a society of a different sort, an older and less rationally ordered society, is found at Kinsale. Kinsale is one of a small group of Irish country towns with substantial numbers of buildings which date back earlier than the nineteenth century. From the thirteenth-century Saint Multose's church onwards, the town has a rich and interesting selection of houses, public buildings, churches, almshouses and military structures filling out the medieval form of the old town. This plan at once escapes the linear concept and you can lose your way in back-lanes and short-cuts, each returning upon itself like the convolutions of a shell. This is the root rather than the node, winding and interlocking and finding itself again.

It is the best point from which to leave or approach West Cork as its architecturally expansive style relates it more to the outside world. Indeed, in political terms, the only points of contact between continental Europe and the south-west of Ireland occurred at Kinsale – with the Spanish – and at Bantry – with the French. However, Kinsale is alone in retaining a feeling of that involvement. Its harbour is defended by a star fort designed by Sir William Robinson, whose Royal Hospital at Kilmainham in Dublin was the first important post medieval building in Ireland. With the Royal Hospital and Charles' Fort in Kinsale, he introduced the spirit of renaissance architecture into the country. The town's Saint Multose's is an intact and living medieval church with later accretions, and the tholsel with its triple, eighteenth-century Dutch curvilinear gables – the last such to survive in the country – offer a more sophisticated visual environment than is to be found further west.

The combination of a safe harbour, the old-world atmosphere of a port town, the historic buildings and associations has given Kinsale an identity which fosters other things. The proliferation of small, smart restaurants in the narrow streets has given birth to a gourmet festival.

Some years ago I had an exhibition during this food festival. The festival was held in October, when tourism was at a low ebb, and its motive was to bring people into the town. The actuality went precisely as planned and the festival-goers revelled, dined and drank their way through the few days of the event. The usual complement of journalists from Irish, British and Continental papers was present to receive some of the perks of their trudging trade. As the days progressed the men and women of the media passed over into a state of hallucinatory good fellowship bordering on euphoria. It seemed certain that they would return to base and publish glowing accounts of Kinsale in their papers. One of the journalists covering culture did an interview with me about my exhibition. It promised to provide excellent publicity.

A year later I met the same journalist at a similar function and asked her what had happened to the interview. She looked embarrassed, sought escape, but then admitted that, well, yes, she did publish it, 'in a way'.

After my interviewer had returned from the gourmet festival she had written a wonderful profile of the artist. Unfortunately, her notes did not record the artist's name, nor could her memory be forced to divulge a clue to his identity. All had been obliterated by good fellowship. At length she got a name; it sounded right, so the article was published. The artist of vision whose name was used happened to be a serious abstractionist and he was not amused. The editor, too, was quite unreasonable, and dismissal was mentioned. However, one must take the long view of these things.

Despite much new orientation and the degree to which improved roads may have altered things, in every West Cork town is embedded the remnants of the village from which it originally developed. The classic nineteenth-century image of Irish village life – single-storey, thatched, whitewashed cabins – are everywhere the genesis of what exists today. Bridgetown in Skibbereen, Staball Hill in Ballydehob, Air

Hill in Schull all have remains of the nineteenth-century village, left behind when the town began to expand in a different direction. Bridgetown in particular is an excellent example of West Cork village architecture of the Famine period. The houses, originally thatched but now slated, climb up the hill from the river, their facades in both single- and two-storey dwellings unplastered, whitewashed stonework. These very cottages appear in a wood engraving published by the London journals in the 1840s to illustrate the appalling conditions of life in the West of Ireland at the time. Apart from one or two which have been tastefully restored they look hardly more comfortable now than they did in the last century. They are so small that it seems scarcely possible that they could have housed such large families. But of course, in terms of habitation, they relate more to the ring fort and wattle hut than to the architecture or society of the industrial era. It is as though late medieval Ireland continued in existence into the modern age. So too did the area's poverty, which clung to its residents long after the rest of the town had prospered.

If these cottages and cottagers represent the end of an era, the churches of the time indicate the opposite emphasis. Wealth and piety, new opportunities and old beliefs, rivalry and pride all combined to produce a riot of church buildings in every town and village of the area and in outlying rural communities. They vary in shape and size, sometimes displaying architecture of the highest order, more frequently the features of an ecclesiastical barn. Yet there is hardly a church in West Cork, particularly the Protestant ones, which does not contain some minor treasure or artistic curiosity from the last three centuries. A good reason for investigating even the most hideous of church buildings is that many contain work by the school of stained-glass artists which constituted one of the undoubted achievements of the cultural revival of the late nineteenth century. Some enlightened rector, parish priest or parishioner of the past may have installed for the greater glory of God, or their own family pride, a bas-relief, a mosaic floor or a window which redeems the repositories of the tawdry and suggests something on a more elevated plane.

For sheer romantic siting Saint Barrahane's church in Castletownshend would be hard to fault. Perched on a rocky escarpment above the village street it has a grandeur out of all proportion to its diminutive size. Bandon likewise has an abundance of churches, all situated for dramatic effect. No matter from which direction you approach the town the view is dominated by one of the many churches rising above the houses. The least ecclesiastical and most interesting externally is the Regency Methodist church, placed right in the centre of the town at the hub of its narrow streets. The architecture is more reminiscent of an assembly room at Bath than a gathering place for Bandon Methodists. Its air is worldly, entirely at variance with the little Methodist chapels to be found in all the other towns and villages. Normally the architectural styles of the Catholic, Church of Ireland and Methodist churches are as predictable as the physical distance between them. While the Methodists are always to be found some-where in the middle, the two larger denominations sit at either end of the town, out of sight of each other if not quite out of mind.

The present era witnesses no less a play of opposing forces. Skibbereen searched for an answer to the modern dilemma of taste with a rummage in the bargain basement of past architectural styles. The main street of the town proudly displays the results of its excursions. Surrounding the Maid of Erin is an assortment of dignified and typical small-town public and commercial buildings, including the Romanesque Revival town hall and the Art Nouveau post office. Then, in the mid-1980s, the Maid acquired a new neighbour, representing an architectural style extinct in Ireland – related, in fact, to an era prior to the emergence of the town itself. The style of the new building, a Savings Bank, is somewhat hybrid, but Tudor interpreted in a Victorian tea shoppe manner would probably best describe it. In a street where the facades slide decorously into one another as smoothly as in ra Georgian square, the tiers of fake Tudor balconies erupt into the street with the violence of a collapsing building. I went into it when it opened, wondering if the perpetrators might have had the imagina-tive grace to ensure that the external impression had been carried through into the activities of the interior. Would there be men in leather aprons, gingham-clad wenches, the hearty laughter of a vigorous peasantry? Nothing of the sort. A clerk in a very neat suit asked me if I would perhaps like to see some brochures.

On the site of an old mill building in the middle of Bantry is the earliest and perhaps the only example of the influence of one of the most significant pioneers of twentieth-century architecture, Le Corbusier, in West Cork or perhaps in the whole of Ireland. Having had a finger in the genesis of this anomaly I must approach it cautiously. The mill-race of the old building takes a sharp curve as it runs around the site of the Corbusian Bantry library. Inspired by the form of a portal dolmen and interpreted in the brutalist manner of the master, this essay in mass concrete outshines the Tudor revival in Skibbereen in affronting the staid dignity of its neighbours. Suspended over the careering stream the massive slabs of the dolmen-library project above and around one in a convincing megalithic manner, and it would not seem out of place to meet a druid coming from the library laden with books about observing the solstice. Approached by a flight of steps, the climb to the building can be an exhilirating experience when the mill-race is in spate and the foaming water gushes beneath your feet. Inside the library all is light and high ceilings like a roofed Stonehenge, and the sheer imaginativeness of the concept overcomes its seeming inappropriateness. Within as without the megalithic motif is pervasive but, unlike the Tudor Savings Bank, there is no sense of the whimsical or the tawdry. Rather, there is a feeling of strength, and it presents a different outcome to the search for an appropriate visual language for West Cork in the late twentieth century. I doubt that it does contain the answer, if taken as a role model, but it is an example of an intellectual rather than a sentimental grappling with the issue and as such is of immense interest.

A Bend in the Road

Main Street, Schull

Pier Road, Schull

Griffin's Bar, Schull

The Eros of Castletownshend

Patrician Houses, Castletownshend

The Old Town, Kinsale

The French Prison, Kinsale

St Multose's Church, Kinsale

The Dutch House, Kinsale

The Stony Steps, Kinsale

The Courthouse, Kinsale

The Smithy, Bantry

Bridgetown, Skibbereen

Air Hill, Schull

Watergate Street, Bandon

The Churches of Bandon

St Maitias Church, Ballydehob

COASTLINE

General wonder in our land,
  And general consternation;
General gale on Bantry strand,
  For general preservation.

General gale our fears dispersed,
  He conquered general dread;
General joy each heart has swelled,
  As General Hoche has fled.

ᴇɪɢʜᴛᴇᴇɴᴛʜ-ᴄᴇɴᴛᴜʀʏ ʙᴀʟʟᴀᴅ

ROARING WATER BAY ENCOMPASSES an area of about a hundred square miles of water between Baltimore in the east and Crookhaven in the west. The tortuous coastline of the bay, as of much of the rest of West Cork, is punctuated by small coves, each with an old stone pier or miniature harbour. Up to the mid-nineteenth century these were the arteries of communication and trade and a wide array of lighters, barges, rowboats and yawls plied the coast, ferrying freight around the rim of the land rather than through it. Never far from the safety of land, they darted from port to port with the assurance of safe harbours at frequent intervals to reduce the threat from treacherous seas. Today, however, only the yachtsman holds this perspective on the land; it is a medieval cartographer's view of the world: good on outlines, vague concerning the interior.

Between the mid-nineteenth century, when road builder Sir Richard Griffiths paved his way from Bandon to Mizen Head, and the arrival of the railways a decade or so later, this coastal orientation was effectively reversed. The Statue of Liberty in New York in 1886 and, a year later, the Eiffel Tower in Paris, symbolized important aspects of the modern world to the inhabitants of both continents. They were beacons for two of the great rallying cries of the time: Liberty and Progress. When the elegant twelve-arch railway bridge on the estuary in Ballydehob was built in the same year as the Eiffel Tower, it must have been equally symbolic to the people of the area. Together with Liberty and Progress, Communication completed a trinity of ideals. The communication and transport of goods, ideas and people were all accelerated by the coming of the railways. Kinsale, the principal town and inlet of West Cork had through centuries dominated by sea travel been in close communication with continental Europe, but now land-based communications penetrated an area which had for the most part been peripheral to all the political, social and cultural developments of the outside world.

Much of the region's railway architecture has been demolished, and the piers and harbours have begun to crumble due to neglect, yet splendid, isolated examples of both still remain like relics of a bygone era. The Twelve Arch Bridge in Ballydehob is one of the finest of the survivors, marching with all the dignity of a Roman aquaduct across the mud-flats of the estuary. A few years ago the centenary of this noble structure was celebrated in the village. A stage replica of the old tram and carriages was produced by a local artist and erected on the bridge. This convincing representation, decorative by day, took on a different aura by night. Floodlit and windswept, far from reminding one of those dear, dead days it suggested the setting for one of the early horror movies – the station below Prince Vlad's castle. In the community hall events were held to commemorate the birthday bridge. The authorities on West Cork trams (which were actually trains) and on Irish bridges regaled the audience with anecdotes of legendary engines and excessive spans. Later, various people rose from amongst the listeners to say that they had genetic links with the railway. All were descended from stationmasters; no scions of firemen or porters declared themselves. A case of natural selection?

As it is one of the most pleasing architectural features of the local landscape, I drew the Twelve Arch Bridge on many occasions and it reappears in a variety of forms amongst these etchings. One village magnate commissioned me to do a large picture of this monument for his new house. The price was agreed and the picture eventually produced. I had chosen an angle which showed the bridge emerging as it does from thickets of brambles and conifers on either side of the water. Delicate fronds of foliage wound in the foreground of the picture and the subject itself basked in the distance, looking solid and ancient. I was quite pleased with the results. When I presented it to my patron he gazed at it in silence for a long time. Then with a large and calloused hand he ran his index finger across the view a number of times, shaking his head slowly as he did so. 'No, no good at all. It won't do,' he muttered more to himself than to me. He had been counting the arches. In my enthusiasm for the atmosphere of the piece the accurately rendered number of arches had become obscured, those on the extreme edges becoming partially lost in the undergrowth. The commission was rejected. If you are paying for twelve arches you don't want to be short-changed with ten and two halves!

The indented contours of Roaring Water Bay enclose a maze of minute inlets and islands. The name derives from a stream which flows down the side of Mount Kidd amidst a landscape of bracken and boulders. The torrent roars in the narrow gaps and gullies as it rushes towards the sea. The little inlets penetrate the land like miniature fjords and create a sense of safe haven from dangerous seas. Their piers, long abandoned except for the occasional fisherman's or tourist's boat, are overgrown and tumbled-down romantic ruins, quiet spots for sighting a lone heron at low tide, grey against grey water. In the narrow defile where the roaring water debouches into the bay nature has done much to reclaim the territory usurped by human purpose. Perhaps, like the closing of a wound, this former embarcation point, which saw many thousands flee a country unable to support them, is being bound in ivy and decorated with wild fuchsia to heal the scar.

Brow Head rises precipitously above the harbour of Crookhaven, a sheet of calm water bounded on three sides by the ragged contours of this curious landscape. The whole prospect seems contorted with nervous energy as rough striations of rock cut through the fields and the cliffs rise up abruptly from the sea. On the summit of Brow Head, commanding a vast sweep of the Atlantic, stands a jumble of ruins. There is no common style nor any co-ordinated plan, yet in different periods all served the same purpose – the rapid communication of news. The tallest of the buildings is the Napoleonic tower, a bleak cube of undecorated stonework perched on the windswept height, the most south-westerly of a chain of signal towers. Dominating the landscape and the sea it could send a message to Dublin Castle in a matter of hours: the Emperor was expected here as elsewhere.

Scattered at its base are later customs and communications buildings. The most interesting of these, although only ruins remain, is Marconi's telegraph station which he operated for a number of years before moving to Knightstown on Valentia Island. During the War of Independence the equipment was smashed to bits in order to prevent messages from being relayed to British troopships off the coast. Today the group of ruins on the headland is a place where sheep may unsafely graze. These historic buildings might still perform some function in the future as a memorial to Ireland's strategic position in transatlantic communications, a sanctuary between land, sea and sky.

From the heights of Brow Head the outline of Rock Island at the mouth of the harbour resembles a partially submerged submarine, its twin customs-observation buildings the conning towers of this strange naval mammoth. An ill-assorted collection of buildings adhere like barnacles to the back of this submarine: the roofless lighthouse barracks, a defunct fish factory and an abandoned, rambling Victorian mansion suggest an unfavourable location. Wedged in the little cove in front of the mansion is the hulk of an old wooden trawler. A graveyard of vanished days and forgotten hopes.

Clear Island lies off the mouth of Baltimore Bay and is, or is reputed to be, a Gaeltacht. Along with two other artists I was invited to come to the island as a guest performer in the autumn festival. We arrived on the mail boat for the occasion, heavily laden with art. I had some twenty large pictures, the sculptor had half a ton of works in steel, stone and wood, and the potter came with three tea-chests of ceramics. A tractor and trailer awaited our arrival and ferried the works to the exhibition hall. I wanted to hang my painting there and then but was told that there was to be a play in the hall that night. 'Tomorrow will be time enough,' I was advised. The following day was a Sunday and the reception was timed for after mass.

That morning things were slow to get moving. The key to the hall could not be found. Children were sent off across the fields to find someone who would very likely have it, and eventually it did turn up. Time, however, was running short, but then the whole occasion – cheese, wine, art and people – seemed to come together all at once. Some art was sold, but after the wine and cheese the islanders began to head home for their dinner. How long would the exhibition run? I enquired, and discovered that it was, in fact, now over. If it went on longer, who would come to see it?

In a moment of quick thinking I asked the time of the next boat to the mainland; the other artists showed no inclination to linger either, so the tractor reappeared and the pictures, ceramics and sculpture were loaded back onto the boat. The whole exhibition had lasted an hour and a quarter. When I arrived back at my studio a letter awaited me, an invitation to be guest artist in Czechoslovakia. Prague is a long way to go for an hour and a quarter, I thought, but then, maybe they do things differently there?

The islands of the West Cork coast are rather grandly referred to as Carbery's Hundred Islands, but only Clear Island and Sherkin now sustain a viable population – though, like the other islands off the west coast, there is a steady draining of young people to the cities on the mainland for education and employment. Horse Island off Schull is evocative of the vanished communities of these islands. Silhouetted against the skyline, this piece of low-lying land appears like an old-fashioned, gap-toothed saw; a dark bulk of rock with triangular projections – the gable ends of a row of roofless cottages – biting into the clouds.

Curiously, most of these islands are almost entirely without trees, the scant good land being used entirely for crops and grazing. But is the windswept location the reason for this bleakness, or is it something else? In Glengarrif the lush gardens of Garnish Island are like a tropical paradise moored off the West Cork coast, with mature trees and an abundance of flourishing plants, and it is no more than twenty miles from the desolate islands of the Carbery's. The difference is perhaps in the fact that Garnish was planted with the long-term view of developing the island as the gardens of a mansion – though the mansion itself was never actually built. Photographs of Garnish prior to its transformation show it as having been as treeless as the other islands are today. In the case of Garnish the initiative was that of a landowner, but the state, which has inherited this mantle, lacks the imagination to plan in this manner. A more inhabitable environment would not have necessarily held the people longer on their sea girt fields, but it might have been helpful.

Baltimore Bay, served by the Ilen river, holds a scattering of small islands. In the town of Baltimore I had one of my wierdest experiences of the bizarre turns taken by human tastes. Sometimes the artist must stretch his definition of fine art to include areas of activity more concerned with earning a few pounds than with pursuing the higher purpose. On this occasion I was engaged to do some painting of the walls and ceilings variety. My employer, a convivial fellow, invited the painting team to stay at his house while the work was being done and, being a hospitable host, the nights were spent in drinking and witty conversation. He himself was quite able to remain up half the night and yet rise early, refreshed and ready for further festive encounters. I wondered as I retired to bed after the first evening how I was possibly going to crawl out of the bed the next morning.

At an early hour on the following day I descended into the first circle of a twentieth-century hell. I woke to a crescendo of marching jackboots. The rousing tones of the Waffen SS chorus thundered the 'Horst Wessel Lied', and the whole house shook as though the entire German Army was about to goose step through my bedroom. Alarmed, I stumbled into the living-room: the marchers were on a record, automatically timed, like an alarm clock, to dislodge even the most difficult guests. Every morning it was like this, until the job was done. The painters didn't linger over their work.

Upstream on the river the main street of Skibbereen forms a U as it follows the bank of the Ilen which loops through the landscape. At the very centre of the town the Caol stream meets the larger body of water running under twin bridges with a slender stone flight of steps descending into the water beneath the arches. This little stream, which runs along the backs of the old nineteenth-century warehouses of the town, struck me as a delightful subject for an etching: water, old stone walls, an assembly of tilting roofs and clap-boarding. Having done the drawing and etched the picture I showed it to a Skibberonian acquaintance. She looked at it in dismay, with an evident wrinkling of the nose and pursing of the lips. 'Why did you have to do that old thing?' she asked testily. Now a stream full of green sedges, it had been the town drain in her youth and she could still smell its pungent odours merely by looking at my picture of it. Needless to say, this particular etching did not achieve much popularity around Skibbereen. Who says that art does not stimulate the senses?

The Estuary of Ballydehob

Clonakilty Rooflines

The Twelve Arch Bridge, Ballydehob

Marconi Station & Napoleonic Tower
at Brow Head

Rock Island & Crookhaven

Boats at Baltimore

Sherkin Island & Schull Harbour

Glandore Harbour

River & Stonework, Clonakilty

The Bridewell, Bandon

Mill Cove, Schull

Gate Lodge at Bantry House

Town & Countryside at Bantry

The Caol Stream, Skibbereen

The Fastnet Rock

UNDER THE HILL

He directs his pure bright eye
along the wall surrounding us,
I direct my clear eye,
Weak though it is, at hard knowledge.

Pangur Bán NINTH CENTURY

FIFTEEN YEARS OF LIVING in West Cork does not make one a native or even a naturalized citizen of the place. This is a fundamental difference between city and country: in the city residence quickly grants one a sense of identity which may not be found in country places even in a lifetime.

To a neighbour of mine I once remarked about a notable village family that to my eye they seemed to be distinguished from their fellow shopkeepers only by their evident zeal for work. My observation was dismissed with a disdainful toss of the head.

'Them, is it?' he spat contemptuously. 'Don't I remember well when his grandfather arrived here with a bicycle.'

You may know every ruin, fence, field and boreen. You may have looked at everything around you, seen much that is invisible to the native and taken note of those things which might soon disappear. You may have an abundance of information on all aspects of the countryside — historical, geographical and environmental — which your neighbours lack. They, of course, don't need it. Your neighbours' knowledge of their own place is at once more real, because it requires no explanation, and more vulnerable, because it can vanish without trace. Which knowledge is more valid: the itemized, observant kind; or that which comes from identifying with a place to the exclusion of all observation? The answer must lie in a blending of these different responses to our common sense of place. In the years I lived in West Cork this synthesis was beginning to take place, with a growing awareness among the local community of its natural heritage balanced by the outsiders' more precise sense of the historical dimension.

A development in the life of rural Ireland which would have been unthinkable only a generation ago is the present existence of communities of artists living in country places far removed from the cities which form the artists' natural habitat. Since the 1960s the villages and townlands of West Cork have been settled in by creative people of many disciplines whose unorthodox way of life is less of an obstacle to communication than it often can be in an urban setting. To the writer, painter, weaver or sculptor, the discipline of the craft imposes long hours of solitary dedication, a situation which must be accepted and can hardly be shared. The basis of most art is formed in a strong core of craftsmanship, and practised repetition finds admirable space for development in a rural environment where the distractions of the ephemeral are minimal. This drift of creative talent to West Cork is not peculiar to this part of rural Ireland; the same phenomenon may be found in other byways of the countryside and, for that matter, in many parts of the western world where city life has become too fraught for all but those whose creative instincts express themselves in excesses of angst. Whatever the limitations of rural life, it is not a breeding ground for angst, and it allows those artists with a more prosaic as well as a more optimistic vision to flourish untrammelled by urban doom or coffee-table culture.

When the gentle values immured in the landscape are seen as defining a world – not one left behind but rather in advance of the commonplace, where some harmony of life and vision becomes possible – then the rural sensibility comes into its own. When I began this series of etchings I responded at first to the individual phenomena in my immediate surroundings. Gradually my horizons grew and I began to include other subject matter until, eventually, a structure emerged from what might otherwise have been a collection of mere views. Categories and themes declared themselves as my eyes became more attuned to the character of the landscape. And as a lifelong enemy of the contemporary artist's lazy habit of working from photographs I found myself much in the streets and fields, drawing. Inevitably, of course, this led to talking with people, and discovering their wonderful capacity to invest everything around them with a human dimension. Every tree and tumbled-down wall had an anecdote attached to it, and these stories merged the day before yesterday with tales of past centuries in an alarming telescoping of time. Although I have concentrated on the physical fabric of the region, behind every shop facade is a face and a story, and the shape of every stony outcrop in a twisted field conjours up the lives of past generations. My etchings are like the shadows on the glass of an old daguerreotype, a hint of what is there; or like a laugh resounding in a narrow street to a story already told and lost.

These are small pictures, each concerned with a limited horizon, and my intention was that they should be accessible to a wider sector of the population than just those with artistic predelictions. They are 'functional art' and as such belong to a venerable tradition of artistic impressions stretching back over many centuries. If they seem to represent a period more distant than the late twentieth century, and show neither slurry tanks nor bungalows, then I must plead that I was seeking essences, essences which are better represented in those things which have stood the test of time.

'Where are you going?' I was asked, as I finished my pint and nodded to the few occupants of the pub.

'I'm going west, to Crookhaven.'

The questioner needed to clarify my generalization. 'Crookhaven is it? That's west of west, the last place in time.'

The Artist's House

The End of the Road

The Lengthy Anecdote

Durrus

Riverbank

Under the Hill

The Book of Life

A note on the etching process

Etching is a method by which a picture incised into a sheet of metal can be reproduced a number of times.

After a drawing has been completed, a sheet of copper or other metal of the corresponding size is prepared. The copper is covered with an acid-resistant film of wax and the picture is drawn with a stylus, a sharp instrument like a needle, into the soft surface of the wax. Then the copper plate is immersed in a bath of acid and the action of the acid on the copper incises the lines into the metal plate. The wax having been removed, the plate is heated, then inked and passed under the roller of an etching press. The pressure of the press forces the etching plate into contact with the dampened paper, and the impression of the picture is passed from one to the other. The image on the copper will not survive indefinite printing so the etchings are produced in limited editions. The process as used today hardly differs from that practised in the seventeenth century by Rembrandt and his contemporaries.

The pictures made in this way are always the mirror-image of what has been etched on the plate, and all the illustrations in this book have in fact been drawn in reverse on the copper. With practice the mind becomes quite used to the convention of drawing a reverse image of what one sees, and it can be done as naturally as drawing directly from nature.

Etchings

COASTLINE

UNDER THE HILL

A NOTE ON THE ETCHING PROCESS